Talking About Civics

I0799256

Heather Price-Wright

Reader Consultants

Brian Allman, M.A.
Classroom Teacher, West Virginia

Cheryl Norman Lane, M.A.Ed.
Classroom Teacher, California

iCivics Consultants

Emma Humphries, Ph.D.
Chief Education Officer

Taylor Davis, M.T.
Director of Curriculum and Content

Natacha Scott, MAT
Director of Educator Engagement

Publishing Credits

Rachelle Cracchiolo, M.S.Ed., *Publisher*
Emily R. Smith, M.A.Ed., *VP of Content Development*
Véronique Bos, *Creative Director*
Dona Herweck Rice, *Senior Content Manager*
Dani Neiley, *Associate Editor*
Fabiola Sepulveda, *Series Designer*

Image Credits: p5 Getty Images/Nitat Termmee; p16 Getty Images/Belterz; p24 Alamy/David Grossman; p29 Alamy/Frances Roberts; all other images from iStock and/or Shutterstock

Library of Congress Cataloging-in-Publication Data

Names: Price-Wright, Heather, author. | iCivics (Organization)
Title: Talking about civics / Heather Price-Wright.
Description: Huntington Beach, CA : Teacher Created Materials, 2022. | "iCivics"--Cover. | Audience: Grades 4-6 | Summary: "We live in complex times, with people asking many questions about what's best for their communities, their country, and the world. Sometimes, these conversations can be difficult. People have strong feelings, and they often disagree. So, how can we talk about civics in a way that helps rather than hurts other people? In this book, you'll learn how to research issues, develop strong arguments, listen to others, and debate in fair and productive ways"-- Provided by publisher.
Identifiers: LCCN 2021054705 (print) | LCCN 2021054706 (ebook) | ISBN 9781087615479 (paperback) | ISBN 9781087630588 (ebook)
Subjects: LCSH: Civics--Juvenile literature. | Citizenship--United States--Juvenile literature.
Classification: LCC JK1759 .P68 2022 (print) | LCC JK1759 (ebook) | DDC 323.60973--dc23/eng/20211206
LC record available at https://lccn.loc.gov/2021054705
LC ebook record available at https://lccn.loc.gov/2021054706

This book may not be reproduced or distributed in any way without prior written consent from the publisher.

Any news source referenced in this book is named for information only and should not be considered as a recommendation from the publisher.

TCM Teacher Created Materials
5482 Argosy Avenue
Huntington Beach, CA 92649
www.tcmpub.com

ISBN 978-1-0876-1547-9

© 2022 Teacher Created Materials, Inc.

The name "iCivics" and the iCivics logo are registered trademarks of iCivics, Inc.

Table of Contents

We Need to Talk

So much is happening in the world at once. Different people have different opinions about how to respond. In your community, or even in your school, there are probably lots of issues on which people disagree. These issues may include who to vote for and what laws should be made. Our lives are full of important questions. Some issues are even bigger, such as how to prepare for the future. There are many possible opinions about all these issues.

These questions are complex. They can also influence our lives in major ways. Because of this, it is sometimes difficult to talk about them without getting a little heated. Debate can be a healthy way to learn and draw conclusions. But as we see every day online and in the media, debates can also lead to anger and mistrust. They can shut down **dialogue** rather than make space for solutions.

Of course, not all civics topics are controversial and debate is not always needed. But when it is, we can engage in healthy, **constructive** conversations. That takes effort. We need to inform ourselves. We need to understand different perspectives. We need to listen to one another. We need to think about our **biases** and our deeply held beliefs. And after all that thoughtful preparation, we need to talk.

Jump into Fiction

Birthday Bash

Charlie could not wait for his birthday dinner. He was turning 12, and the whole family was gathering to celebrate. He and his dad had spent all day cooking his favorite foods—barbecued ribs, corn on the cob, and even homemade potato puffs. His older sister Angie was bringing chocolate cake. Aunt Susan and Uncle Mike would bring their famous rolls and potato salad. Mom even said he could have soda, which was a real treat!

Everyone was in a great mood when they sat down to eat. His mom said grace, and then Charlie immediately started digging in. His dad passed around the ribs, proudly telling everyone he had made the barbecue sauce from scratch.

"Did anyone watch the candidates for governor debate the other night?" Angie asked. She followed politics closely and loved to have lively talks about current events. "There were lots of interesting ideas! I'm not sure yet who I'll vote for."

To Charlie's surprise, Uncle Mike made an angry sound under his breath. "You can't trust any of that," he growled. "The media lets them say whatever they want. One candidate made it sound like we should all feel ashamed of our history. It's a disgrace!"

"I didn't hear anyone say that!" Angie retorted. "What I heard was that we need to be more open and welcoming to each other."

"Please," said Charlie's mom. "Let's talk about something else. It is a party, after all!"

But they kept going. Uncle Mike hissed, "We're not paying attention to what's right under our nose! It's bad for the country!"

Angie's eyes flashed. "You don't know what you're talking about!" she shouted.

Charlie had been listening wide-eyed. But now it was time to speak up. "Hey, everyone, I'm really glad you're here for my party. I want to know what you think. But maybe we can say things in ways that remind us that we like each other. All right?"

Angie looked at Charlie, smiled, and tousled his hair. "You're right, kiddo. Sorry. Guess I got a little caught up, didn't I?"

Uncle Mike was red-faced. “You caught me, kid. I wasn’t really listening, was I? Start again?” he asked, looking at Angie.

“You bet, Uncle Mike,” Angie said with a smile. “So, what did you think about the debate? I’d love to hear your thoughts.”

“Me too, Angie, me too. I really do want to know what you think. I know I’m set in my ways, but as Sue here often reminds me, there are more opinions in this world than mine,” he chuckled sheepishly.

Charlie looked around at his big, awesome family. They didn’t always agree, but they knew what mattered. When all was said and done, they were better together. And together on his birthday was exactly where Charlie wanted to be!

Back to Nonfiction

Know Your Stuff

We have all had arguments with people that seemed to go nowhere. That may happen when neither person is well informed. **Productive** conversations are based on facts and research. We cannot rely on feelings and opinions. Of course, it is fine to feel strongly about an issue. It can be worthwhile to try to correct things that seem **unjust**. But the best way to do that is to fully understand the issue.

Reliable Sources

How can you find the facts you need? The answer might seem easy. After all, so much information can be found on the internet. But you cannot believe everything you read online. For example, a site such as Wikipedia often has good basic information. However, researchers have found many examples of bias in its articles. There are more articles about famous men than similar women. The majority of its articles cover more recent events, too. So, it may not be the best source for historical facts.

Think and Talk

How do you know if an online source is trustworthy? What can you do to be sure?

Who Wrote It?

Another potential example of bias on Wikipedia is in who writes the articles. Most entries are written by people in Europe and North America. This can impact how people learn about the rest of the world. It is important to seek out diverse sources.

Reading the news is a great way to learn about important topics. But you should also pay attention to where news stories come from. Different newspapers, magazines, and websites have different points of view. It is best to find a variety of articles on one topic. That way, you are getting many **angles**. For example, one article on an upcoming election could tell you what candidates think about one issue, such as education. Another article might describe the backgrounds of the people running. A third story might report on how much money each campaign has spent. And still another article could tell you who the writer thinks you should vote for.

These all may be good things to learn. But they are best when put together. Then, you can get a clear picture of the election. You'll know what the candidates think. You'll know who supports them. You'll understand what resources they have. And if many sources report the same thing, you will have a good idea that you can trust the information. Think about how much more accurate your conversations about an election would be if you had all these details!

Checking Sources

Online sources can be tricky to **validate**. There are a few things to look for to help you know a source is reliable. Is there a named author for the article? Is there a date for the article? Do other reliable sources report similar things? These are pretty good indicators that the information is reliable.

Facts and Opinions

Imagine you are reading what you thought was a regular news article. But then you realize the author seems to tell only one side of the story. This can be a **jarring** experience. After all, we want reporters to be **objective**.

Opinion writing is an important part of media. It lets people share their ideas. This can help us make sense of complex topics. Other people's opinions are also a good way to challenge our own thinking. It is important to know when you are reading an opinion piece.

What clues can you look for to know if something is opinion writing? Writers won't always say "in my opinion." Instead, look for words that show there might be multiple ideas on a topic. You might read that someone *claims* or *argues* an idea. These are words that express a point of view. Or a writer might share a personal experience when making a case. This often means it is a piece of opinion writing. If you find yourself getting angry or upset as you read, that can also be a good sign that you are reading an opinion.

Personal experiences can help guide our thinking. But they should not replace facts. Hearing others' opinions is a healthy part of learning. Just be careful to identify them as opinions. Then, think critically about the claims being made and the ideas being expressed.

Not everything printed can be trusted as real news.

"Fake News"?

Fake news was originally used to describe misleading stories published on social media. Now, this term is occasionally misused. Some people use it to describe news they do not like or do not agree with.

Well-Informed

Now you've learned to review a topic you care about. How do you put that knowledge to use in conversation? It is all about being clear and fair. Calmly state the facts you have learned. Share what conclusion those facts have led you to. Then, listen to the other person's thoughts and respond.

For example, maybe you looked into your community's plans to build a park on some public land. You learned that some people want the park but others want it as a nature preserve. An endangered species lives there. Some people say that the species and people can coexist in the park. Others say that people in the park will destroy the species' habitat and put it in even more danger. You read opinions about the issue and looked for the facts behind them, too. You confirmed the facts and found balanced, fact-based evidence. You can now have a conversation with others about the topic. You can share your thoughts and back them up with your research.

Of course, having good evidence will not always stop a conversation from turning into a fight. People feel strongly about important topics. That is why it is important not only to do research but also to practice healthy communication skills!

Headlines can be misleading because their goal is to grab attention. They should not be used as facts in an argument.

No Comment

Have you seen a news story with the sentence, "This person could not be reached for comment"? News reporters work hard to be balanced. They reach out to everyone discussed in an article to get their points of view. If someone does not want to talk, the reporter will still make sure readers know they did their job by reaching out.

Keep Your Cool

Talking about important issues is not just about knowing the facts. For one thing, it is usually possible to gather evidence for both sides of a story. One reason civics can be so difficult is that different opinions can be equally **valid**.

So, what do you do when you can't convince someone of your point of view and you can't agree with theirs? First, take a deep breath. It is great to be passionate about a topic. We should care about things such as our government and our rights! But be careful not to let that passion turn to anger. Not only does it not feel good to lose control of your emotions, but it will also make the other person less likely to listen to you.

Active listening can go a long way in keeping discussions positive.

Practice saying things that demonstrate you are hearing the other person. Even if you disagree, showing that you are listening goes a long way. When the conversation gets heated, take a pause. Say, "I appreciate your point of view. I know we both care a lot about this." That will remind you and the person you are talking with that you are not trying to hurt each other. You are just expressing yourselves.

Active Listening

Use your body to show someone you are listening to them. Maintain eye contact, and avoid fidgeting or shifting around. Nod your head and smile when you hear something you agree with or to show the person you hear them. Repeat what you hear to show understanding. And ask questions when you have them!

Understanding Bias

Our understanding of the world is shaped by what we see and hear. Family, friends, neighbors, religious communities, and school play roles in someone's thinking. So do the things you watch, listen to, and read. People learn many things from these sources. They learn how to treat people fairly and do what is right. But sometimes, they also learn things that seem like facts but are opinions. That is because every environment produces biases. Everyone is biased. The important thing is to pay attention to your own **preconceived** ideas. This will help you understand others' beliefs and opinions, too.

Think and Talk

What are some biases you have?

Maybe you were taught that it is always better to read about something than to watch a TV show about it. You have unlimited time to read books. Your house is full of them. However, television time is very limited. This might create a bias. You now believe that the ideas in books are more likely to be correct than those on TV shows or on news programs. Imagine you find yourself in an argument with someone for whom television is their main source of information. You might be more likely to ignore their arguments. In a case like this, it is important to identify and understand your bias. Listen carefully. Do not assume the other person is less informed.

Implicit Bias

People have biases they do not even know about. These biases are referred to as implicit. Implicit bias can cause negative views about many things, including different races and genders.

Practicing Empathy

Have you heard the saying that you have to walk a mile in someone else's shoes to understand them? It is not talking about footwear. Instead, this expression describes empathy. This is the ability to understand and take into account others' feelings and experiences. Empathetic people are able to imagine how others feel, even if they have not had the same experiences. That often makes them kinder and more open to different perspectives.

Empathy is not a superpower like mindreading. Anyone can do it! And it is one of the most important skills to **cultivate** if you are going to talk about big issues. People bring their own backgrounds and experiences to any debate. If you can empathize with those experiences, you can understand them better. All it takes is practice. When you are talking with someone, try to see things through their eyes. Maybe you ask your friend what he had for dinner last night and how he liked it. Now, imagine you ate what he did and felt as he did about it. This might feel like a silly exercise. But growing your empathy skills will help you in all kinds of ways.

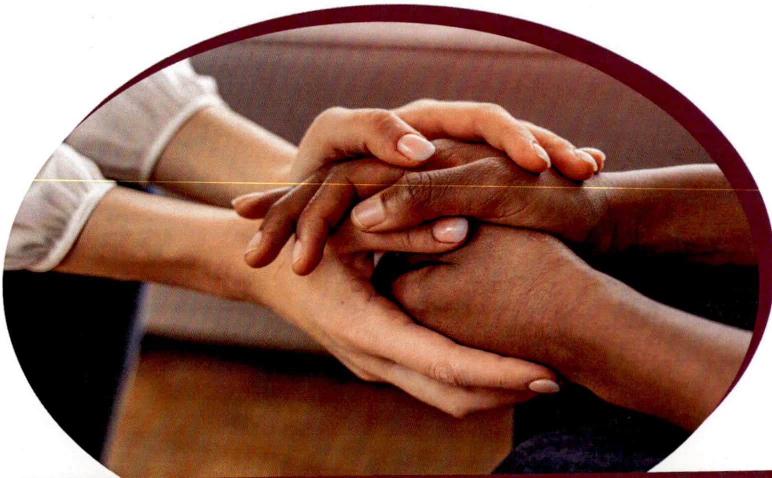

People can build their empathy through practice.

Crowding in communities can be a topic for debate.

Read All About It

Looking for an easy way to walk in someone else's shoes? Pick up a book! Studies show that reading fiction can boost empathy. People who read are better at picking up on others' feelings.

Let's look at a harder example. Some people in your neighborhood are angry about a new apartment building. It will be much taller than any other buildings nearby. Many people will live there, which means more garbage, more people using the local park and playground, and new students in the local schools. Some adults feel that this building will make the neighborhood a less pleasant place to live.

Maybe you agree with them. But then you meet a kid whose family hopes to move into the building. The conditions where she currently lives are not great, and the new place will be better for her and her family. She will also get to go to a neighborhood school, which has classes she can't take at her current school.

Exercise your empathy. Imagine you lived with lots of people and had very little space. Can you imagine wanting there to be a home your family could afford? Think about how it would feel to know some people do not want your family to live nearby. They are worried you will make their neighborhood worse. Is that a good feeling?

Even if you have not changed your mind entirely, empathy has helped you. You have a broader perspective and better sense of others' feelings. This is never a bad thing!

Think and Talk

Should you use empathy even if people you are working with do not?

Lifelong Learning

There are many pieces of the puzzle when it comes to talking about civics. Good conversations should involve solid facts and open minds. At their best, these conversations can open your eyes to new ideas. They might even change how you see things! Our **polarized** culture gives the impression that people who change their minds are weak and unable to stick to their convictions. In reality, learning new things *should* sometimes cause you to develop new opinions.

People anywhere and from all walks of life can be certain only they know what is right.

It is a difficult balance to strike. Perhaps you have strong convictions, or beliefs. Sticking to those **fundamentals** can help you make good choices and treat people well. At the same time, no one has all the answers. Life is a learning journey, and you should treat new information as an opportunity. Does it challenge something you thought you understood? Does it help you see an issue in a new light? Does it uphold your previous belief or **contradict** it? You are confronted with many chances to shift your perspective or to find better support for your beliefs. Take advantage of them!

The Backfire Effect

People *really* do not like to have their strongest beliefs challenged. In fact, our brains respond to ideas that contradict our strongest opinions in the same way they would to physical threats. This can cause us to dig in our heels when faced with new information. People have to work hard to overcome this impulse.

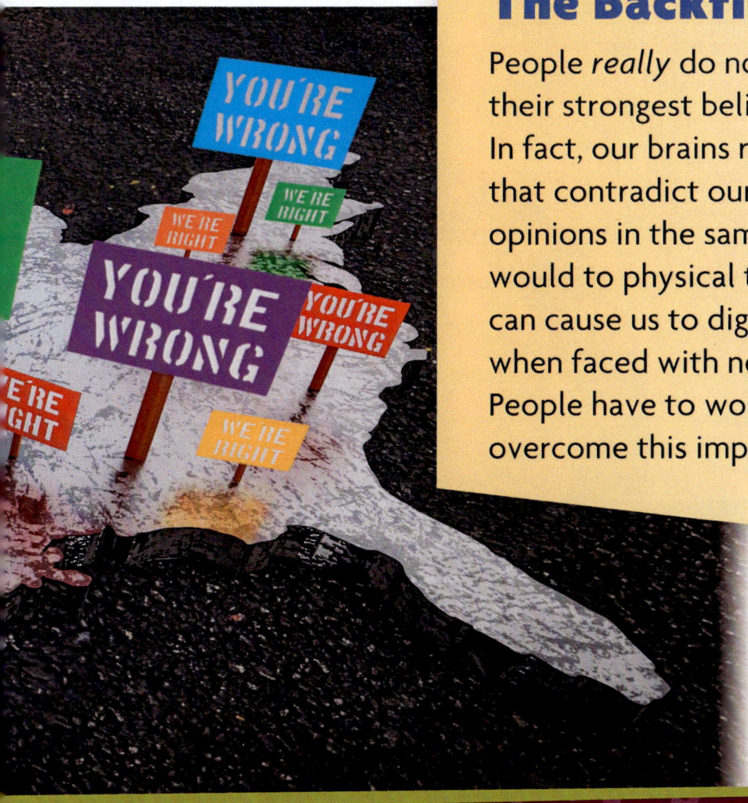

Having fair and well-informed conversations about civics will **enrich** your life. It will allow you to learn from others. It is also a great way to **hone** your own research and debate skills. Most importantly, it will set you up to participate in a democracy. Conversations with people in your community will help you make decisions, such as who to vote for. You can decide what to look for in a candidate. You can look into both sides of **ballot** measures. You can practice persuading others to support the same things you do. You might even get involved in a campaign or volunteer for an issue you care about! The ability to make strong arguments and listen to others will help you throughout your life.

Living in a democracy comes with many precious rights. But people also have the responsibility to be active and well informed. That means they should have skills to talk to people who agree with them *and* people who do not. People should be prepared to base their beliefs on facts. They should defend the beliefs they hold dear. But also, they should strive to understand others' perspectives. And this journey never ends. As we grow as people, citizens, and leaders, we must deepen our understanding of our world and how to talk about it.

Debaters support different solutions or sides of an issue.

Glossary

angles—particular ways of approaching or considering certain issues

ballot—a piece of paper used to vote in an election

biases—prejudices in favor of or against certain things, people, or groups of people

constructive—serving a useful purpose

contradict—say the opposite of a statement

cultivate—to improve or develop a skill or habit

dialogue—conversation between two or more people

enrich—improve or make something better

fundamentals—the basic and important parts of something

hone—to improve or refine something

jarring—having a harsh or unpleasant effect

objective—based on facts rather than feelings or opinions

polarized—divided into two groups or opinions that strongly disagree

preconceived—formed before having actual knowledge about something or before experiencing something

productive—achieving good results

unjust—not fair or morally right

valid—fair or reasonable

validate—confirm to be true

Index

Civics in Action

It can be hard to talk about tough topics. Of course, civics topics are not always controversial, but they can be. It may feel easier to avoid them. But it is helpful to learn how to discuss these tricky topics. You can help others learn how to do so as well!

1. Reread this book. Look for the "dos and don'ts" for evaluating information, sharing opinions, responding to someone, and making people feel comfortable.
2. Create a how-to poster for kids with tips for talking about tough topics.
3. Share your work!
4. When you have a chance, put your tips into practice.